COCKTAIL MIXOLOGY

For Medical professionals

And you!

Party bar, hydration station.

Create your own to infuse tasty mixes,

the possibilities and

concoctions are endless.

*Free bonus #1 in the back of
your book is a historical timeline
of "History of Alcohol" pg.122

***Dedicated to
EVERYONE affected by Covid19
a.k.a. Coronavirus,
the survivors and
those not so lucky.

BY: Marilyn Ryan

Pharmacy Technician by day
Mixologist by night

COCKTAIL MIXOLOGY

For Medical professionals and you!

Published by Kindle Direct Publishing

Are you responsible if your guest leaves your party drunk or even sober?

If they get drunk and are involved in an accident?

<u>*Host liability is determined,*</u>

<u>*by state law.*</u>

Social host liability refers to a party host, who serves alcohol, being held legally responsible for the actions of intoxicated guests.

Make sure *never* to serve minors alcohol.

Do not let them drink in your home then drive.

Some states will hold the host or homeowner responsible, if your guest drive drunk after leaving your home.

Keeping this in mind, have a key dish by the entry way as guest arrive. Ask guest if they will put their car keys into the dish upon a arrival.

Ask them if they drink too much would they want to stay at your place? or call a cab? A friend, family member, what do they prefer. It may help if you have several guests to make a note of the preferences with a name of who they want to call and the phone number as well.

This way before they start the party you know their preference and they know you're not letting them drive drunk.

At the end of your visit, or party decide how to move forward with the keys. You give the keys back if you feel comfortable.

Otherwise look back at your notes, take care of your friends and family, this is all part of having fun responsibly.

Stay safe and enjoy your party. Cheers!

I am dedicating this book
to all the people affected
by Coronavirus.

The survivors, as well as
those that did not
survive.

This has been a terrible, yet
eye opening pandemic. Our
world will never be the same.
Maybe that is a good thing in
many ways. We have all come

together in directions people
never dreamed of.

Let's honor those people that
gave their lives to this
Coronavirus. We can do this
by keeping this sense of
community all over the world, in
the days, weeks, months, and
years moving forward after we
conquer this virus.

I say *after we conquer this virus*
because I am writing this book
during the pandemic. My work
hours were cut in half therefore
I am filling in my time writing
this book. I am one of the
fortunate ones.

Millions of people are out of
work around the world.
Businesses have closed; our
economy is suffering. We are
required to wear face masks
and practice social distancing.

If you are reading this year of
2020 when I started writing or
2021 when I actually publish,
social distancing means people
are to stay 6 feet or more apart.
No shaking hands or friendly
hugs to someone you run into
that you haven't seen in ages.
This is especially hard for me I
am a hugger.

I met my cousin Richard
yesterday at the store and
wanted to give him a big hug,
but we can't do that at this time.
Usually when you greet
someone if you don't hug you
shake hands especially in
business meeting situations.
Not these days.

We will make it thru these times
and have a better world in days
to come.

I first had this book idea last year. You know how it is with many ideas, they just sit in the back recesses of your mind then pop up again to tickle the brain.

I hope you will enjoy reading this information as much as I am enjoying putting this book together.

Thanks for taking the time to read my work.

Sincerely,

Marilyn Ryan

INDEX

COCKTAIL

MIXOLOGY

For Medical
professionals

And you!

INDEX Continued:

of mixology (also known as) Drink Recipes.

INDEX BOOK BONUS:

BONUS Quarantini DRINK DUE TO TIMES WE ARE SURVIVING TODAY.

. Blank pages for your personal notes to add to your

book for future generations to enjoy and try. Pssst. Maybe be nice and leave a blank page or two for your future generations to add some notes they can pass on as well! Remember to always date the notes.

CHAPTER 1

Basic hydration station bar set up

Gather your preliminary prep instruments,

and tools!

Beakers or Glasses

Stir rod or long bar spoon for stirring liquids.

Mortar & Pestle or bowl and muddler stick

Graduated cylinder or measuring cup.

Cocktail shaker A common measuring tool is a "jigger" A jigger has a cup on each end.

The smaller end is ¾ oz. known as one half jigger.

The other end is   larger it's known as a full jigger it holds typically

1 ½ oz. of liquid.

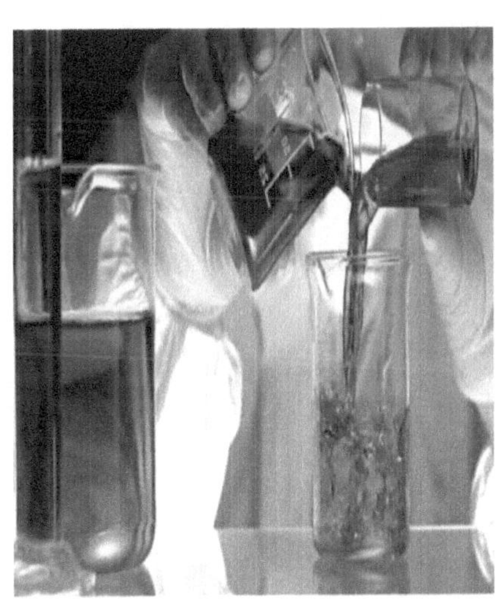

Bar tender ~ mixologist and medical chemist have this in common, they all use formulas to *"do the math"* in whatever they are mixing.

Here is a formula that will help you decide how much of each mixer item you may need have on hand to stock your bar.

There are 25 ounces or an average of 16 shots in a 750-milliliter bottle; Use this to estimate how many bottles of each ingredient you need.

Ice is a must have when stocking your bar. Sounds simple like duh… However, there are many types of ice to choose from. Crushed ice, cubed ice.

Some people also fill fun shaped ice cube trays the day before the party then freeze them. You can use food color in your water then fill the ice cube trays. This makes a funky splash of color. Especially if you are having a color theme to the party.

I like to put a piece of fresh herb, mint or some other cute leaf in my ice cube trays then freeze them. These frozen herbs look lovely in the drinks as a garnish. They may add a bit of flavor twist as the ice melts.

If you only purchase one type
of ice, use cubes. You can
always crush the cubes in a
blender should you need to.

I like to save time by
purchasing a bag of crushed

ice just to have on hand in the freezer on standby. Do it your way it's your party.

In our next chapter we will decide which mixers and alcohol type to stock up on. Of course, you will keep your preferred flavor on hand, but you should also have one or two other types to offer friends and family.

Not everyone has the same taste. Bonus this saves your favorite flavor for you to have another day if guests are drinking something you don't prefer but keep on hand for variety!

CHAPTER 2

Alcohol, Mixers

& Garnish options

Here in chapter two we have a list of the basic types of alcohol infusion options that are miscible to keep on hand, in stock for your bar set up.

Have you ever heard the term top shelf alcohol?

Top shelf refers to the quality and price of the alcohol. Usually the more expensive products are at eye level and above in the store. Hence the term "top shelf".

The cheaper bottles are usually found on the lower shelves in the liquor stores as well as most other stores that sell alcohol, elixirs & tonics.

Top shelf is not always a better quality. In some types of alcohol, it really does make a difference, but in others not so much.

Cheap liquor has been referred to as rot gut because the fluid burns going down. It's not a pleasant burn, I had to try it. Once was enough.

Of all the alcohols it is my opinion top shelf matters the most with Tequilas. You may have a different experience or opinion. I enjoy hearing about your experiences, so do my readers. That being noted feel free to share your advice and experiences on my website:

All I ask is you keep it friendly to help teach others.

Ugly comments need not be shared. Thank you in advance.

WHAT ARE THE DIFFERENT TYPES OF ALCOHOL?

Tequila

You should buy a good brand. Splurge on a 100 percent agave tequila. Why splurge on

100 percent agave? Because the cheaper brands of tequilas have a *nasty* after taste no juice can disguise. Yuk!

You will find tequila sold as gold or silver. Gold has been aged in oak barrels. Silver or Blanco is used within 2 months of distillation. It is young.

Either is fine whatever you prefer. Margaritas are usually made with silver. It has a stronger flavor and mixes well

Cheaper tequila also contains more corn syrup and grain alcohol. What's bad about that combination? Evil hangover… enough said.

Vodka

You will find many brands
available. Choose the best
deal because vodkas in general
don't have a bad flavor like
tequilas can. You can save
here to use the extra savings to
splurge on your tequila.

Bourbon

Spend a bit more for a middle
or top shelf bourbon. I'm not a
bourbon expert, personally I
prefer rum. I am told that
cheap bourbon has a burn
sensation as you swallow it.
The better bourbons are
smooth.

Some people like to drink bourbon straight over ice, no juice or soda mixers.   In this case the smoother the bourbon slides down the throat the better your experience with the drink will be. Either pleasant or causing a cough and hack side show.

Rum

Now we are talking! This is my flavor. Rums are complex. There are so many variations to rum. I always buy a good middle or top shelf rum. You want to a smooth light sugary flavor, not a cheap skanky flavor.

Rums can be mixed with almost
anything. Soda, juice or just
served chilled over ice. This is
the most popular alcohol used
in blender style drinks.

Scotch

Splurge on this spirit. It is
almost always served over ice
or to use the slang term "*on the
rocks*" Remember you always
stock cube ice also known as
the rocks.

Some people drink it straight, this means no ice / rocks. Just straight up.

Brandy & Cognac

Both are made from grapes. The difference is Cognac is distilled more times than Brandy. Most brands are good whichever shelf they sit on until they are added to your bar.

Gin

There are many varieties of Gin. They are actually made with an assortment of ingredients.

Not a standard same ingredient in all types of gin.

Usually at our house we use Hendricks Gin.

Why? Simply because my husband Bruce loves cucumber basil martinis you MUST use Hendricks Gin for this it matters.

The ingredients in Hendricks Gin work best with that drink. It has infusions of rose petals and cucumbers in it.   We tried & experimented with cheaper brands to save money and trust me. It matters on this drink. Other drinks it may not matter, use your taste preference.

Moonshine

Is homemade, unaged whiskey, usually it is clear color, with a corn base and high alcohol content—sometimes peaking as high as 190 proof.

Wow!

Traditionally, it was produced in a homemade still and bottled in a mason jar.

Although historically it was sold illegally people still made it to sell and drink personally.

Some people still make this at home using the still method even today.

My husband & I have brewed our own beer before it may be fun to make a still. Hmm, new project….

Whiskey

Shop for whiskey the same way you would your scotch. This is also served on the rocks or straight up. You want to serve a smooth whisky not one that burns the throat and stomach.

Whiskey comes in many forms. Some are flavored, bold, light, dark. Taste a few and see what you prefer.

** Hey here's an idea! **

If you're not into whiskey, maybe your just not familiar with it, I know it's' not my preferred flavor. I'm more of a rum and vodka lady. Why not have a taste party? Invite friends over.

Each friend brings a bottle, and you all take turns trying the variety. This can be done with any of the spirits that I have talked about so far.

Rum tasting, Vodka tasting.
Gin tasting, Tequilas, you get it.
We have all heard of wine
tastings so why not try
something new.

If you do have a taste party,
please go to my website and
leave a comment letting me
know what you chose and how
well it went over. Everyone
would love to see that update,
especially me.

What were your favorites?

Why did you or your friends
prefer them?

Mixers

Tonic water, seltzer water or
club sodas & juices should
always be a good brand. They

can have a bad after taste that can overpower the flavor of the alcohol if you cheap out.

These are the base mixer of many alcohol drinks. After spending money on the liquor, you don't want to cheap out on the mixers and ruin the drinks.

Fruit juice and soda can also be used as a mixer.

We watch our sugar intake at our house; therefore, we use diet sodas and sugar free juice. Alcohol already turns to sugar in your system. We use the sugar free mixers when available.

We have also used water with crystal light or equivalents as a mixer. My Nephew Cody and his wife Courtney shared that tip with us when we were hanging out the night before a friend's wedding.

Oh yes, It's delicious. It was very tasty. I can almost see you shaking your head no way water with crystal light. Just try it.

Colas and ginger ale are the most popular sodas for mixers.

Cream and or milk can be used as mixers. Several common cocktails (for example white Russians) require milk, half-and-half, or cream.

It's also ideal to keep some vanilla ice cream behind the bar for very creamy cocktails. This helps chill the drink and make it smooth.

Living in Florida we have lots of cold icy drinks… Yummy.

Are you ready for a drink yet? I am!

PAUSE ****************

**** Ok, I'm back drink in hand,

   Ready to keep working on

this book for you. I am drinking a Quarantini. What's that? Keep reading you'll see.

Cocktails

What is a Cocktail?

A *cocktail* is an alcoholic mixed drink, which is either a combination of spirits, or one or more spirits mixed with other ingredients such as fruit juice, flavored syrup, or cream.

There are various types of *cocktails*, based on the number and kinds of ingredients added.

Did you know that Cocktails have cousins called Mocktails?

Well, they do. Mocktails are actually *non-alcoholic* drinks.

They have their own chapter. They deserve a chapter, delicious!!

Serve them in cute glasses and no one know they are alcohol free except for the mixologist of course.

This will help the designated driver not feel left out or make them stand out at the gathering.

MOCKTAILS

What are Mocktails?

They are non-alcohol drinks.

Delicious and refreshing drinks.

Sans the booze.

A cocktail without the liquor, using juices, sodas, infused waters and many other non-alcoholic ingredients to provide flavor and color.

These Mocktails can look and taste just as delectable as their cousins Cocktails, without the buzz.

The Mocktail formulas and compounds deserve their own chapter. See Pg. 106

Recap:

Cocktails have alcohol in them.

Their cousin Mocktails do not
have alcohol in them.

Garnish

Deliciously &
attractively

Your garnish makes a huge difference, don't leave it out. Always plan to have a garnish in the pantry & fridge.

It can be as simple or elaborate as you feel like making it,

Always use a bit of flair

Lemon sliced into rounds, wedges, spirals.

You can also slice the peel thin then twist it hang off the side of the glass. Dip in sugar first if you want a sparkly fancy fairy tale look.

Lime can be used the same as lemons above.

Orange can be used the same as lemons & limes.

Olives. Some mixologist use black olives the most popular are the green olives with pimentos inside.

Stuffed olives on a stick, skewer or toothpick are a popular choice as well. I will have a recipe for that in the recipe section of this book.

Celery.

 Mainly it is used in bloody Mary drinks and a few other drinks as an edible garnish.

Adding colored salt takes it up a notch.

Cherries

Cinnamon grated on top of creams.

Mint or herbs, remember those ice cubes? Freeze a bit of herb in a cube.

Pineapple sliced or wedged.

Salt, usually a coarse salt, the coarser salt can be seen, therefore it's more decorative.

If your event has a color theme, then you can add a bit of food color ahead of time to the salt. Make sure to let it dry then you're ready. Probably do this colored salt a day or so ahead of the event so it has time to dry.

Pink Himalayan salt

Pepper

Strawberry

Blueberry

Blackberry

Raspberry

Watermelon, any kind of

melons, as you know melons

are tasty and come in colors.

Cantaloupe has a peachy pink
color Honey Dew melons are
green

* Watermelon hint: Huge oval
watermelons will be watery and
not s flavorful as smaller round
watermelons. If you see brown
crusted lines on the top it just
means the bees pollinated the
fruit flower multiple times. It's
not as pretty but boy is it sweet
and tastier, go for the ugly

round watermelon, she is a hidden gem. I live in the South we know our watermelons.

Bitters is an alcoholic mixture flavored with botanicals creating a bitter sour flavor. You can make your own or purchase bitters premade for your bar set up.

**I have a recipe on pg.

102 of this book, it'll

teach you how

to make your own bitters.

<u>CHAPTER 3</u>

Party formulas ideas and toasts

In this short chapter I am going to toss out a few party ideas.

Like I said back on page 35, Why not have a taste party?

Invite friends and family over. Each friend brings a bottle of their favorite spirit and you all take turns trying the variety available.

This works with wine as well if you prefer wine to stronger alcohols.

You can make a numbered list of the type of liquid / brand / also guest's name.

Have that guest's number on a
separate sheet of paper, tape
the number over the bottle
label. Now it's a mystery.

Make sure that all your guest
have been admitted, then
checked in. Bottle logged in &
then labeled.

When your fully staffed, bring
out the liquid / solutions / elixirs
/ drinks and glassware. Shot
glasses or solo cups whatever
your party theme is suited for.

At a Pharmacy party we would
use empty pill bottles as shot
glasses. Ask your local
pharmacy for a few empties
they will probably share them
free.

As each guest takes a taste or
shot of the options have them
write / chart the number of what
they like best and least.

If your guests are still standing when the tasting is over you can have them compare charts preferences, likes, dislikes all the above.

It's fun to examine the charts to see how people's taste are similar or different.

For your hydration stations I am compounding a mega mix list of ideas below.

Use one idea or infuse several ideas to brew up an incredibly funtastic party.

The party your friends will talk about for years to come. It'll make headlines on Instagram, Facebook, twitter, snapchat all of the socials!

As you greet your guest at the door have a tray of preliminary prep shots to offer them. Get your party started off with zest and effervescence.

Most of you are familiar with standard jello shots, recipe will be in the "formula ingredients/ recipes "chapter of this book for the how to make a jello shot pg. 107

One fun twist on the standard jello shot that is usually in a small dose cup is to pull them up into liquid syringes for oral jello *shots*.

Another party favorite is to serve "shots" in mini glasses. Label the serving trays with a few different fun descriptors.

- Probiotic shots
-
- Specimen shots
-
- Oral shots
-

- Hydration station shots
-
- Apothecary shots
-
- Admixture shots
-
- Miscible shots
-
- Phase transition shots
-
- State of matter shots
-
- Proportional shots
-
- Tonics
-
- Use movie titles
-
- Use animal types
-
- Any other name you like, some people get creative, some get nasty, or funny, by now you get the idea, just have fun with it.

**Snacks always have
some munchies nearby.**

Choose your food and snacks to serve according to whatever theme you have started for your party. If it's indoors or outdoors.

Your possibilities are endless.

Some people feel hesitant to invite a crowd over to the house.

No worries your friends won't judge your clutter we all have a bit of clutter. Some of us more than others.

It's the memories you make with family and friends that matter.

You will be remembered for those memories, not the junk drawer in the kitchen.

Here's a little secret almost EVERYONE has a junk drawer, some people have two. (Guilty)

Enjoy life, make the most of your time use it wisely to create those unforgettable memories.

Here are some delightfully fun toasts you can share with each other…

"Salud" (is Spanish for health, wealth & security)

"Cheers" (is English for health, wealth & security)

"Hip Hip Hooray"

"Bottoms up"

Or if you feel chatty here are some with a few more words…   "To your health"

"Here's to the nights we'll never remember with the friends we'll never forget."

"To friendship"   "To family"

"Over the lips past the gums look out tummy here it comes"

"There are fast ships, slow
ships but best of all are
friendships, here's to smooth
sailing in a friendship with
me"

"One bottle for four of us!
Thank God there's no more of
us!"

 "To my friends, willing, loyal
and able. Let's start drinking!
Everyone C'mon get your
glasses off the table!

If you have any amazing toasts
to share, I'd love for you to
leave them in a comment on my
website so I can enjoy them as
well as others.

https://relax-live-enjoy.com

__CHAPTER #4__

Apothecary journal

Of

mixology

A.K.A.

(also known as)

Drink

Recipes

QUARANTINI

A drink invented in 2020

during

coronavirus/covid19

{ INGREDIENTS }

4oz of Pedialyte (preferred)
or orange juice

2 oz of vodka

lime garnish

Intermingle the
ingredients in a glass,
garnish with a lime,
then enjoy the
refreshing does of
electrolytes, voila!

SHAZAM ADMIXTURE

{ INGREDIENTS }

6 oz Rum

1 can of Frozen Pina Colada
Mix

1 can of Frozen Strawberry
Daiquiri Mix

Infuse $\frac{1}{2}$ the rum with the
pina colada

Blend the remaining rum into
the Daiquiri

Phase transition first the pina
colada into a glass,

then pour / titrate with the
daiquiri on top of pina colada,

garnish as desired

Shazam Enjoy!

PINEAPPLE ZINGER

** *Warning***

Only for those that can handle their liquor Lightweights stick to rum and coke

{ INGREDIENTS }

1 fresh pineapple

1 full bottle vodka

Combine the 2 ingredients, cover let it sit 3 to 7 days, strain out the fruit serve over ice.

Garnish as desired based on what kind of fruit you used.

Sip this do not swig or chug it!

Continued on the next pg.

Tip:

Use a good top to middle shelf vodka, not the dirt-cheap stuff.

This tip applies to tequila also.

Actually especially tequilla, the bottom shelf cheap stuff has a nasty after taste that will ruin a good drink. People that know anything about alcohol can spot the cheap stuff at a snif, before they even taste it, beware…

I have heard some people swap the Pineapple out for mangos or peaches. Almost all fruits make a lovely addition to your masterpieces. Enjoy.

Blazen

{ INGREDIENTS }

4 cups of vodka or tequila your
pick

2 cups cinnamon red-hot
candies

Ice

Crush the candy, into a teeny
tiny pieces or powder.

Add candy to the liquor, seal
the top.

Continued on the next pg.

Then let it absorb and
comingle.

The flavors together for several
hours.

The longer it sits the better it
will taste.

Then enjoy over ice!

Tip: cute cubes if made with red
food color.

A make ahead before serving
at a party.

ISLAND SUNSET

By the pitcher full

{ INGREDIENTS }

8 cups or 64 oz. Pineapple juice

5 oz. of lime juice

8 cups or 64 oz. Coconut Rum

5 oz. Grenadine

8 cups or 64 oz. Lemon-Lime soda

Fresh pineapple pieces to float in pitcher

*Also use pineapple to garnish each glass of Island Sunset

Continued on the next pg

If you don't want a full pitcher of Island Sunset

4 oz. Pineapple juice

2 tbsp. lime juice

4 oz. Coconut Rum

2 tbsp. Grenadine

4 oz. Lemon Lime soda

Fresh pineapple slices

THE PAIN KILLER:

If you have ever been to the Caribbean or on a cruise ship you have probably enjoyed one of these drinks. This is one of my personal favorites.

PAIN KILLER

{ INGREDIENTS }

2 oz. Pusser's Dark Rum

4oz. parts pineapple juice

1 oz. part orange juice

1 oz. part cream of coconut

Pinch of ground nutmeg

Orange and/or pineapple wedge or maraschino cherry for garnish.

HOT TODDY

This is an old-fashioned drink,

Believed to help relieve cold &
cough symptoms.

Helping you to feel warm and
comfy inside.

{ INGREDIENTS }

1 cup of hot water

2 oz. whiskey

2 to 3 tsp honey

2 to 3 tsp lemon juice, to your
taste

Stir together then

Garnish with a slice of lemon
Continued on the next pg

Optional

- Some people like to add 1 oz. apple cider

•

- Or a cinnamon stick

•

Sip slowly covered in a cozy blanket

&

With rest you'll feel better soon.

BLOODY MARY

* One of my husband Bruce's favorite

6 oz of tomato juice or V8 juice

Small splash of Worcestershire sauce

A squirt of lime for lemon juice

3 oz. Vodka

Then give it a Swish & Stir

If you like it spicy add a dash of tabasco sauce,

Another swish & stir

Pour over ice,

Dash of black pepper on top

Garnish with a celery stick,& cute straw

OLD FASHIONED

{ INGREDIENTS }

2 tsp simple syrup

1 tsp water

2 dashes of bitters

1 cup ice cubes

2 oz. bourbon whiskey

1 orange slice

1 maraschino cherry

Pour the simple syrup, water,
and bitters into a whiskey glass.

Stir to combine, then place the
ice cubes in the glass.

Pour bourbon over the ice.
Continued on the next pg

Garnish with the orange
slice and maraschino
cherry.

ENJOY!

ALMOND JOY

{ INGREDIENTS }

1 OZ. Cream of coconut

1 OZ. Amaretto

1 OZ. Dark crème de cacao

2 OZ. Cream

Fill mixing shaker with ice, pour
above ingredients over ice

blending them together then…

Shake it, shake it, shake it….

Strain liquid into a highball
glass filled with ice,

garnish as desired,

Enjoy!

CUBA LIBRE'

**(COMMONLY KNOWN
AS RUM & COKE)**

{ INGREDIENTS }

2 OZ. Rum

6 oz. Cola

Combine these 2
ingredients over ice,
enjoy!

*For people that don't
care for dark soda*

try this variation:

CUBAN COOLER

{ INGREDIENTS }

2 OZ. Light Rum

6 OZ. Ginger ale

Combine these 2 ingredients over ice, enjoy!

Remember the Garnish - with a lemon twist

FUZZY NAVEL

{ *INGREDIENTS* }

2 OZ. Peach schnapps

6 oz. Orange Juice

Orange slice

*Fill a glass with ice,

add the peach schnapps

then the orange juice, stir &

garnish with an orange slice

*If you don't like sweet
orange juice drinks,

switch it up into a

FUZZY FRUIT

1   ½ oz. Peach schnapps
5 oz. grapefruit juice
(unsweetened)

Mix
same as above

GROG

(An Irish drink)

{ INGREDIENTS }

2 oz. Rum

1 sugar cube or 1 tsp of
sugar (1cube is = to 1 tsp)

1 Tbsp. lemon juice

2 cloves

1 cinnamon stick

Combine all ingredients in a
large mug

Add a little bit of boiling water
Stir together until sugar cube
dissolves, Garnish with a lemon
twist

MIMOSA

{ INGREDIENTS }

3 oz. Orange juice

3 oz. chilled champagne

dash of triple sec or
Cointreau * optional

Combine above ingredients into
a chilled glass, stir gently,&
enjoy!

Since this is a 50/50
proportional drink it may be
adjusted to titrate up or down in
volume, based on personal
taste & quantity desired.

Make this drink by glass or
by the pitcher full.

BART SIMPSON

{ INGREDIENTS }

½ oz Premium Whisky

½ oz Amaretto

½ oz Peach Schnapps

Splash of cranberry juice

Fill a shaker with ice and ingredients

Shake then strain into a chilled glass, enjoy

NOTE *This an exception to my garnish rule, it's awesome alone without a garnish.

FROZEN PUMPKIN MUDSLIDE

{ INGREDIENTS }

2 oz Vodka

2 oz Kahlua

2 oz Irish Cream

8 oz Vanilla Ice Cream

8 oz Pumpkin puree

1 tsp Pumpkin pie spice

Whipped cream

Chocolate syrup

This is more of a after dinner dessert drink!
Continued on the next pg

*A clear glass is
decorative & prettier
with this drink.
This way you can see
the chocolate lines.*

Blend the first 6
ingredients together,
if you don't want to count
no worries just know
that's everything
except the whip cream
and chocolate syrup.

Drizzle the chocolate
syrup into the inside of a
glass, in lines.

Pour the frozen pumpkin
mudslide into the glass
where you just made
chocolate syrup lines.

Top with whipped cream,
add a straw, serve, enjoy!

One of my personal favorites! I know you've read that on another page.

Hey, a girl can have more than one personal favorite!

{ INGREDIENTS }

2 oz Tequila (I use mid to top shelf)

2 to 3 dashes of lime juice

3 oz Orange juice

½ oz Grenadine

Fill a high ball glass or a clear glass with ice.

Add Tequila & lime juice.
Continued on the next pg.

Top this with orange
juice, Stir,

Pour grenadine down a
spoon let it rise from the
bottom of the glass down
the spoon. **DO NOT
STIR** Very cool
presentation if you don't
stir it.

The grenadine will infuse
with the other ingredients
s l o w l y like a
sunrise….

Simple, yet professional
looking, you will look &
feel like a mixologist
when you serve this one
to friends and family.
WOW! Oh, ah, ah!

YELLOW FEVER

{ INGREDIENTS }

2 oz Vodka

4 oz Yellow lemonade

Fill a glass with ice

Add vodka

Add lemonade

Stir

Garnish with a slice of lemon

Enjoy!

GOOMBAY SMASH

{ INGREDIENTS }

1 oz. spiced rum

1 oz Coconut Rum

1.2 oz Crème de banana

2 oz Orange juice

2 oz Pineapple juice

Blend and serve in a

hurricane glass,

garnish with pineapple slice

or orange slice,

go wild use one of each!

COSMOPOLITAN

{ INGREDIENTS }

1 oz Cointreau

1 oz Lemon juice

2   oz Cranberry juice

2 oz vodka

Mix with ice in a shaker.

Pour the mixture into a cocktail glass

Garnish with a slice of lime

JEZEBEL

{ INGREDIENTS }

2 oz. Southern Comfort

2 oz. Baileys Irish Cream

Layer into a shot glass,

Enjoy

JAMAICAN DREAM

{ *INGREDIENTS* }

151 Rum

Tia Maria

Pineapple Juice

Mix equal parts of all three
above ingredients

Shake with ice

Strain into a shot glass

Your equal parts can be at
your discretion, depending
on the final volume desired.

Ladies & gentlemen it
doesn't get any better that
this!

SCREWDRIVER

{ INGREDIENTS }

2 oz Vodka

4 oz Orange juice

Mix together

Pour mixture over ice in a

glass, stir, enjoy

SEAHAWKER

{ INGREDIENTS }

Blue Curacao

Vodka

Midori

Layer equal parts into a
small glass

Quantity of equal parts is
based on final

Volume desired

WHITE RUSSIAN

{ INGREDIENTS }

2 oz Vodka

1 oz Kahlua

Splash of cream

Combine these 3 ingredients

Shake in mixer shaker cup

Pour over ice in a glass

Garnish & enjoy!

WINE COOLER

- *Have you ever wanted to make your own wine cooler?*
- *Here is how it's done …*

{ INGREDIENTS }

Your choice of wine,

red or white

I usually use a sweet wine
not a dry one

ice

7– UP

Continued on the next pg.

Fill a tall glass with ice,

Fill it ¾ of the way up with
wine

Fill the rest of the way to
the top with 7-UP

Stir and swirl around

Garnish with a twist of
lemon or lime

The original Arnold Palmer

3 parts sweet tea

1-part lemonade

¼ part rum

(Exact ratio measurements
depend on total volume
desired, glass, pitcher,etc..)

For a Modern Arnold Palmer

Some people changed the ratio
over time if you prefer it this
way ask for a

Arnold Palmer half & half

½ sweet tea

½ lemonade

Go ahead live dangerously,
experiment see which way you
like it best.

TEST TUBE BABY

{ INGREDIENTS }

1 oz Vodka

½ oz Sambuca or Triple-sec

Cream

Combine Vodka &

Sambuca or triple-sec

Into a large shot glass

or a tall narrow glass

Continued on the next pg

*The type of glass is where
the "test tube" look comes in.*

*Narrow is best to keep the
theme.*

Place a straw into
cream, put your finger over the
end.

Remove straw from the
cream keeping your finger
on the end.

Place the cream filled straw
into the glass until it touches

The bottom of the glass,
release your finger

Serve, enjoy!

CUCUMBER BASIL MARTINI

4 oz. *White* cranberry juice

2 oz. Hendricks Gin (It matters
pay for Hendricks, splurge)

1 oz. triple sec

1/2 oz. light green Martini Rossi
in the bottle

1 cucumber

2 basil leaves

Peel the cucumber, cut up,
reserve 2 cucumber wheels for
garnish, put the rest of the
cucumber pieces into a mortal
pestle or other muddler cup
crush the peeled cucumber and
basil leaves together.

Add the liquids,
Continued on the next pg.

shake well,

strain bits of fruit and herb basil
over a glass of ice,

garnish with cucumbers

serve with a straw

* We talked a cruise line
bartender into sharing his
secret recipe then I modified it
a bit to our taste. We hope you
enjoy this refreshing cocktail as
much as we do here on our
warm Florida evenings, as we
sit outside on our patio.

** I can usually only find my
white cranberry juice at ABC
liquor store or Wal-Mart stores,

I am not endorsing either of
these I'm just sharing facts of
the shopping locations since it
is not easy to find everywhere.

EGG NOG

Traditional holiday recipe

{ INGREDIENTS }

1 Dozen Eggs

2 cups fine granulated sugar

1-pint Jamaican Rum

1-pint cognac

3- pints whole milk

1-pint cream

Nutmeg or cinnamon , both if you like them

Separate eggs * save egg whites in a separate dish. Beat yolks and sugar until thick. Continued on the next pg.

Add rum, cognac, milk and
cream

Stir mixture

Set aside and chill mixture in
the refrigerator

When ready to serve do NOT
add ice cubes

Beat the egg whites you saved
earlier and fold them into the
egg mixture. Do NOT beat, just
fold gently Pour into glasses
sprinkle with nutmeg or
cinnamon,

Serve cold, enjoy. Store
remaining eggnog mixture in
the refrigerator until ready to
drink. Makes approx. 25 to 30
servings.

BITTERS

From the medicine cabinet to the home hydration station bar, bitters have been known down thru history to play a part in healing ailments, as well as, flavoring drinks.

Bitters may appear to be mysterious, at heart, bitters are merely aromatic bitter herbs and spices infused or tinctured in spirits.

Blending the various flavors of the herbs are where the fun part comes in.

So let's, make some homemade bitters, get your mixology on!

Lemon-Lime Orange Bitters

{ INGREDIENTS }

4 Oranges

1 Lemons

1 Lime

1 tbsp. gentian root pieces

½ tsp fennel seeds

½ tsp coriander seeds

½ teaspoon whole cloves

2 cinnamon sticks

One 750 ml bottle of vodka

Continued on the next pg.

Directions:

Steps to make Bitters:
Follow this formula …..

Heat oven to 200
degrees. Using a
vegetable peeler, peel the
lemon, lime and orange to
make zest strips, do not
to remove pith.

Place the zest strips on a
parchment paper lining on
a baking sheet then bake
approx. for 1 hour. This
is to dry the zest strips
out. Remove from the
oven and let the zest
strips cool down.
Continued on the next pg

Place the cooled zest
strips into a one-quart
glass jar then add the
remaining ingredients on
top of the zest strips.

Cover tightly and store in
a cool, dark place for
three weeks, shaking jar
once a day.

After the 3 weeks is up
then pour the liquid
through a fine mesh
strainer or paper coffee
filter and into a clean jar.

Add your zest strips
discarding the other
pieces of aromatics.
Continued on the next pg.

When stored in a cool, dark
place, bitters will keep up to six
months.

Don't forget to note expiration
date on your bitters,

the same as you would any
other type of infusion,

for emulsions, solutions, or
solids.

CHAPTER 5

MOCKTAILS

Q: What are Mocktails?

A: They are non-alcohol drinks.

Delicious and refreshing drinks.

Sans the booze.

A cocktail without the liquor, using juices, sodas, infused waters and many other non-alcoholic ingredients to provide amazing flavors.

Your Mocktails can look and taste just as delectable as their cousins Cocktails, but without the alcoholic buzz.

They deserve their own
chapter, don't you agree?

Recap:

Cocktails have alcohol in them.

Their cousin **Mocktails do not have alcohol** in them.

Keep reading for a few Mocktail

Formulas to try yourself

or for the kids.

Mostly for the party's
designated driver!

*hint

Kids love to have these drinks
served into fancy glassware
just like us adult's use.

It makes the drink feel special
for them.

So, like I always say, "don't
forget the garnish!"

That's right even for the kids!
They actually love to add their
own choice of garnish.

It really does make a
difference in the enjoyment of a
drink.

Arnold Palmer Mocktail

This is an extremely popular summer Mocktail.

It is named after a famous Golfer Arnold Palmer. He used to order this after playing his golf game.

A simple combination of iced tea and lemonade infused together.

Arnold Palmers have the best refreshing taste.

People love to drink them poolside, as well as, on a trip to the beach.

The original Arnold Palmer

3 parts sweet tea

1-part lemonade

Modern Arnold Palmer

Some people changed the ratio
over time if you prefer it this
way ask for a

Arnold Palmer half & half

½ sweet tea

½ lemonade

Go ahead live dangerously,
experiment see which way you
like it best.

(Shhh... Some people spike it
with rum changing it into a
Cocktail)

Shirley Temple Mocktail

A Shirley Temple is a non-alcoholic mixed drink, or Mocktail, traditionally made with ginger ale and a splash of grenadine, garnished with a maraschino cherry.

Modern Shirley Temple recipes sometimes substitute lemon-lime soda or lemonade.

I remember this drink as a little girl. When I would go out to eat with my parents and they ordered me a Shirley Temple it was always served in a real glass and looked like an adult beverage. I felt so special and grown up.

I bet many of you do this for your kids as well. It was not something we ever made at home it was only for special dinners out in a restaurant. It is a nice memory, so I wanted to include it in this book hopefully you will make memories with the children in your family. Your own kids, nieces, nephews all of the crew.

SHIRLEY TEMPLE

Grenadine syrup

Ginger ale

Maraschino Cherries

Ice

Pour the ginger ale into a glass over ice, add a splash of grenadine syrup, and do not stir. Let the splash of grenadine float around on its own. Garnish with a cherry on top and a straw, serve.

Peach Bellini Mocktail

First fill a glass with ice,

Then pour over ice 1 Cup of
Peach juice

Add 1 Cup of ginger ale on top,
do not stir.

Float a few pieces of fruit on
top to garnish

Serve with a straw, enjoy

Butter beer,

Just as good that kind Harry
Potter and his friends enjoy!

1 ½ cup brown sugar
2 tbsp. water
6 tbsp. butter
¼ tsp of salt
½ tsp apple cider vinegar
1 cup heavy cream, divided
3/4/ tsp. rum extract
4 (12 oz) bottles of cream soda

In a pan over medium heat,
combine the brown sugar and
water. Bring to a boil and cook,
stirring often, until the mixture
reads 240°F on a candy
thermometer.

Stir in the butter, salt, vinegar
and 1/4 of the heavy cream.
Set aside to cool to room
temperature. **Continued on the
next pg**

Once the mixture has cooled,
stir in the rum extract.

In a medium bowl, combine 2
tablespoons of the brown sugar
mixture and the remaining
heavy cream. Use an electric
mixer to beat until just
thickened, but not completely
whipped, just a few minutes

To serve: divide the brown
sugar mixture between 4 tall
glasses (about 1/4 cup for each
glass). Add 1/4 cup of cream
soda to each glass, then stir to
combine.

Fill each glass almost to the top
with the bit of extra cream
soda, add whipped topping
over each. Enjoy.
Abra~Delicioso!!

Swamp Juice Mocktail

4 cups Orange Kool-Aid or
Orange colored juice

3 cups pineapple juice

2 cups white grape juice

9 drops orange food
coloring

Serve over Ice, if desired
unless you make this ahead
and It is already chilled.

Since we live in gator
country here in Gainesville
Florida, home
Continued on the next pg.

Of the UF Gators we
always garnish this with a

blue fruit, blue berries, with
blue straws, or
orange.anything blue or
orange. GO GATORS!

Best if served in a clear
glass to enjoy the colorful
pop of orange & blue Gator
colors. It is a great game
day drink.

Of course, you can always
switch this up from a
Mocktail to cocktail.

I think you can figure out
how that is done.

A bit o` rum, or a bit vodka,
mmm. Mm. Mm.

Virgin Bloody Mary Mocktail

1 cup of tomato juice or V8
juice

Small splash of Worcestershire
sauce

A squirt of lime for lemon juice

Then give it a Swish & Stir

**If you like it spicy add a dash
of tabasco sauce,**

Another swish & stir

Pour over ice,

Dash of black pepper on the
top

Garnish with a celery stick,

Serve with a straw

Jello Shots Recipe

Ingredients

1 3-ounce package gelatin.

1 cup boiling water.

1/2 cup flavored vodka.

1/2 cup cold water

Mix above ingredients together, pour into small cups "shots" chill in the refrigerator until firm,

then enjoy

A brief history

of the

alcohol

we enjoy

and

love today

800 B.C.
Barley and rice beer are produced in India.

3000 B.C.
Beer and wine are produced in ancient Egypt.

4000 B.C.
Wine making is established in Mesopotamia (which is present day Iraq).

8000 B.C.

In Middle East, a fermented drink is produced from honey and wild yeasts.

1789
The first American temperance society is formed in Litchfield,

Connecticut, with the goal of
reducing alcohol consumption.

1906

The Pure Food and Drug Act is
passed, regulating the labeling of
food and drink containing alcohol.

1910

New York introduces the first drunk-
driving laws.

1920

The 18th Amendment (prohibition
effectively outlaw the production,
sale, and transportation of alcoholic
beverages in the United States

1920-1933

The illicit alcohol trade booms in the
United States.

1933

Prohibition is repealed; most states restrict youth under 18 (the minimum voting age) from possessing or consuming alcoholic beverages.

1935

Alcoholics Anonymous is established; the American Medical Association passes a resolution declaring that alcoholics are valid patients.

1980

Mothers against Drunk Driving is established

2000

A new federal law requires states to pass legislation making it a crime to drive with blood alcohol concentration (BAC) at or above .08 percent.

***

*MY DOCTOR TOLD
ME, I REALLY
NEEDED TO
STARTWATCHING
MY DRINKING.*

*SO, NOW IM OFF TO
FIND A BAR WITH A
MIRROR IN IT.*

***

*A FRIEND SHARED
THIS WITH ME ONCE.
I STILL FIND IT
FUNNY:*

***

Alcohol is not in my vodkabulary. However, I looked it up on whiskeypedia and learned if you drink too much of it, it's likely tequilya.

***

Thank you for buying, reading and hopefully using this book to make life a little festive.

If you enjoy this book consider buying copies as gifts for friends and family.

Salud, Cheers, Hot damn and all that good stuff, have an amazing rest of your day.

Best regards,

Marilyn Ryan

A link to my Author page:

https://www.amazon.com/-/e/B08NQ3828H?ref_=pe_1724030_132998070

Other books I have written, available on Amazon

E-Books

Paperback books

Books By Marilyn Ryan

The following pages are reserved for your own recipes. thoughts and party ideas:

DATE:

Recipe shared by:

RECIPIE:

DATE:

Recipe shared by:

RECIPIE:

DATE:

Recipe shared by:

RECIPIE:

DATE:

Recipe shared by:

RECIPIE:

DATE:

Recipe shared by:

RECIPIE:

DATE:

Recipe shared by:

RECIPIE:

DATE:

Recipe shared by:

RECIPIE:

DATE:

Recipe shared by:

RECIPIE:

DATE:

Recipe shared by:

RECIPIE:

DATE:

Recipe shared by:

RECIPIE:

DATE:

Recipe shared by:

RECIPIE:

DATE:

Recipe shared by:

RECIPIE:

DATE:

Recipe shared by:

RECIPIE:

DATE:

Recipe shared by:

RECIPIE:

DATE:

Recipe shared by:

RECIPIE:

DATE:

Recipe shared by:

RECIPIE:

DATE:

Recipe shared by:

RECIPIE:

DATE:

Recipe shared by:

RECIPIE:

DATE:

Recipe shared by:

RECIPIE:

DATE:

Recipe shared by:

RECIPIE:

DATE:

Recipe shared by:

RECIPIE:

DATE:

Recipe shared by:

RECIPIE:

DATE:

Recipe shared by:

RECIPIE:

DATE:

Recipe shared by:

RECIPIE:

DATE:

Recipe shared by:

RECIPIE:

DATE:

Recipe shared by:

RECIPIE:

DATE:

Recipe shared by:

RECIPIE:

DATE:

Recipe shared by:

RECIPIE:

DATE:

Recipe shared by:

RECIPIE: